TAMING THE WELLING EMOTIONS:

Dealing With Anger And Hate In Your Life

Godfrey Hunt

Table of Contents

INTRODUCTION

Although they are two sides of the °same coin, hatred and anger do not always have the same components. One may be fleeting, while the other develops and lasts for a longer time. The fact that both emotions are poisonous to the bearer and the target, however, is a given. Like love, anger and hatred are two psychological urges or feelings that are shared by all humans. Both of these urges have negative or painful experiences as their basis. Because of this, whether something bothers us or makes us upset, we as humans often experience anger emotions for just a little amount of time before finding a suitable solution. On the other side, hatred is a strong negative emotion that lasts longer and deeper than anger and has the potential to result in much worse things like retaliation and grudges.

I have yet to meet a person who has never engaged in one of these two interests as a recipient or disher. But we need to figure out how to handle them if we want our relationships to become better. You have probably heard that anger not only negatively impacts our economic well-being but also our physical health.

In this book, we shall examine the emotions individually, deal with anger, and then examine hatred.

Chapter 1: A Look At Why We Get Angry

People perceive events differently, thus a circumstance that angers you could not anger someone else at all for example, other reactions could include annoyance, hurt, or amusement. But just because we all have our interpretations of events doesn't always imply that your interpretation is incorrect if you get angry.

Numerous aspects of your life might influence how you perceive and respond to a situation, including: your background, upbringing, experiences from the past, and present situation.

Thinking about how and why we perceive and respond to circumstances may help us learn how to better manage our emotions, regardless of whether our anger is directed at something that occurred in the past or something that is now taking place. It may also assist us in developing effective coping mechanisms for our anger.

The way we understand and respond to certain events is what leads to feelings of rage. Everyone has their own unique set of circumstances that set them off, but some typical ones include: threatened, assaulted, frustrated, or helpless, feeling invalidated or unjustly treated, or as if others don't value our emotions or things.

Sometimes the source of your current anger may not only be the circumstance you are in right now, but also a former experience. If this is the case, the amount of anger you are experiencing now may be a reflection of a previous event.

If you were unable to express your anger at the time because of specific historical experiences that made you furious, such as abuse, trauma, or bullying as a kid or more recently as an adult, you may still be dealing with those angry sentiments now.

You may have seen individuals you trusted act violently when they were angry, which taught you that anger is dangerous and harmful. This may indicate that you are now terrified of your rage and feel uncomfortable expressing it when anything gets you upset. Then, for some reason that can be difficult to understand, those sentiments could come up again at a different moment.

If you currently have a lot of troubles in your life, you can notice that you become irritated more often than normal or at irrelevant topics.

You can discover that you vent your anger at other times if a certain issue is making you upset but you don't feel able to deal with it directly.

Grief may also include anger. It may be quite tough to deal with all the contradictory emotions you could be experiencing if you've lost someone close to you.

Maybe, you didn't learn how to comprehend and control your furious sentiments because you were brought up believing that it's always OK to express your anger forcefully or brutally. This might imply that you often lose your temper when you don't like how someone is acting or when you're in an unpleasant scenario.

Maybe, you were taught as a youngster that you shouldn't complain and that doing so would result in punishment. This may indicate that you tend to repress your anger, which might cause you to respond improperly to novel circumstances in which you feel uncomfortable over time.

Our Body and Anger

Anger is a feeling that we experience both physically and mentally, like other emotions. In actuality, when we feel furious, a complicated set of physiological reactions take place.

The amygdala, a pair of almond-shaped brain regions, is where emotions mostly start. The area of the brain known as the amygdala is in charge of detecting dangers to our safety. When dangers are detected, the amygdala emits an alert that prompts us to take protective measures. Since the amygdala is so effective at alerting us to dangers, it causes us to behave before the cortex, the area of the brain responsible for cognition and judgment can assess whether our response was appropriate. In other words, we tend to act before fully considering the effects of our actions because of the way our brains are constructed. This is not a justification for terrible behavior; with little work, you may learn to manage your violent urges. Instead of being a talent we are born with or something we can do naturally, it implies that we must learn how to control our anger appropriately.

Your muscles stiffen up when you grow irritated. Neurotransmitter molecules are produced within your brain, giving you a short-lived energy boost that may last for several minutes. The typical furious impulse to take quick protective action is driven by this explosion of energy. Your blood pressure elevates, your heart rate quickens, and your breathing rate quickens all at once.

As more blood flows into your arms and extremities in preparation for physical exertion, your face could flush. Your focus becomes focused and fixed on the object of your rage. You will soon be able to focus only on it. Additional brain neurotransmitters and hormones, including adrenaline and noradrenaline, are quickly released, resulting in a protracted state of alertness. You are now prepared for combat. Your prefrontal cortex, which is a part of your brain that is situated just below your brow, can manage your emotions even if they have the potential to go amok. The prefrontal cortex manages judgment and the amygdala manages emotion. Your emotions may be turned off by the left prefrontal cortex. It performs an executive function to maintain order.

Being aware of this may assist us in discovering safer and less stressful ways to react to current circumstances.

Learning techniques to assist your prefrontal cortex to dominate your amygdala can help you gain control over your ability to respond to sensations of rage. While we prepare our resources for a battle during the physiological preparation phase of anger, it also includes a wind-down phase. When the object of our rage is no longer reachable or in danger, we begin to relax back into our resting state. But it's hard to calm down after being enraged. Our anger threshold is lowered by the prolonged, adrenaline-induced arousal that happens during the rage, which makes it simpler for us to get furious again later. We do quiet down, but it takes a very long time for us to go back to where we were while we were sleeping. We are more inclined to react violently to tiny irritations that otherwise wouldn't bother us during this gradual cooling-down time.

The Dark Side of Anger

The inability to control your anger might also lead to mental health issues. Your ideas and emotions are impacted by anger. When you're upset, you can attempt to forget what made you angry or use alcohol or other drugs to lessen your anger. In most cases, using drugs to fix issues just makes things worse. Additionally, anger impairs your capacity to think properly, which may lead to poor judgment and unwise judgments. You could even say something that you later regret.

Energy surges brought on by anger cause your heart rate, blood flow, and muscular tension to rise. Adrenaline also enters your system during these energy surges. Your heart health suffers if you lose your anger. When it is continued, it may shorten your life. Your immune system is also compromised by anger. Everyone has moments of rage, but learning to manage it well may help you maintain good health.

The same residual arousal that keeps us poised for additional outbursts of rage may also obstruct our capacity to recall the specifics of those outbursts with clarity. Arousal is essential for effective memory.

Arousal levels that are moderate support learning and improve memory, focus, and performance. However, there is a maximum amount of arousal that is advantageous to memory, and when arousal reaches that maximum level, it makes it more challenging for new memories to develop. Your capacity to focus is greatly reduced when you are experiencing high levels of arousal, such as when you are upset. This is why it is hard to recall specifics from highly heated debates.

Chapter 2: Taming Anger

We have always been told that certain things are unchangeable. A mountain cannot be movable. The ocean cannot be dried up. You can't alter your brain, etc. When you are furious, consider if your degree of anger and how you are responding to it is in proportion to the cause of your anger. Have you gone too far? Are you aiming your rage in the right direction? Do you have a personal agenda? It is far preferable to monitor your emotional state throughout the day and deal with your emotions before they go out of hand. Check-in with yourself to see whether your muscles are beginning to tighten up and your heart is starting to race. All of them serve as signals.

The greatest sages, from Buddha to Mark Twain, have attempted to convince us that passion is more harmful to us than anything else. Therefore, we must actively work to control our wrath.

Understanding Anger Problems

Even while having a little bit of rage is natural and good for you, having trouble controlling your anger may be hazardous. Take note of your angry patterns and, if required, get assistance. You could have problems controlling your rage if you: Are you physically or verbally abusing others? You're always getting furious, feeling out of control in your fury, when furious, you often regret what you said or did. Be aware of the minor or trivial things that aggravate you.

It's crucial to recognize the symptoms of rage difficulties and comprehend how to deal with them. This guards you against deterioration of your mental health, physical troubles, and relationship concerns.

The news and happenings in your environment today might be overwhelming, perplexing, and infuriating. This may cause furious outbursts that harm your way of living. So how can you tell if you have anger management problems?

Take Note

Outbursts are common among people with anger management problems. As a kind of mental health illness, anger may worsen and include abrupt outbursts of violence, impulsivity, or disruptive conduct. When you have anger management problems, you may accidentally smash things, hurt people or animals, get angry on the road a lot, or have temper tantrums. This has a bad impact on your relationships, job, and academics. Additionally, it can have legal repercussions.

Typically, aggressive outbursts are accompanied by:

- angry actions
- becomes elated or hyper
- easily aggravated
- flustered thinking
- shaking\tingling
- the report of chest pains
- rapid breathing or palpitations

Explosive verbal and physical outbursts may be expressed via berating, slapping, shoving, heated debates, physical battles, property destruction, and assaults on people or animals. Learning to control your anger or to calm down is thus essential.

Imagine if your errors and failures from the past kept coming back to mind. If that's the case, you'll probably feel disappointed in yourself. You may get more irate if you have ongoing grudges and are constantly annoyed by other individuals or situations. Learn self-forgiveness so you can move on from your past. To assist you in moving ahead, spend some time figuring out the root causes of your anger.

One indication that you have rage problems is that you hate yourself. Knowing what brings on this unpleasant mood and comprehending its potential causes and intensity can help you find a solution.

Other red flag include easily becoming discouraged by the News. While being forceful may help people overcome injustice and anxiety, furious outbursts often include physical retaliation, which leads to aggressiveness. It's essential to ground self-talk and distance oneself from the cause while dealing with this problem.

Also, being judgmental is a response to the wrongdoing or deficiency of another person. It might be challenging to maintain composure while speaking with someone who is giving you trouble if you are quickly annoyed. Find alternatives and express disagreement without being patronizing or demeaning to others. Find out how to manage your rage in a relationship by:

- Putting your words aside and let the other person speak.
- Identifying any signs of rage in your body language
- Listening
- maintaining a safe distance

Various sexes may exhibit different forms of anger difficulties. The same holds at various ages. View the examples below to see if you can identify any of the warning indicators of anger management issues:

You often instigate fights.

You constantly assign blame.

You maintain that your actions are acceptable because others around you are overly sensitive. The brain now tries to explain away the undesirable behavior.

You have a hard time expressing your feelings, except for becoming furious to regain some control.

Your aggressive actions give you the impression that you can dominate others.

When you're around, you notice that your friends, family, or coworkers seem uneasy or as if they're treading water.

When you lose control of your rage, you inadvertently harm other individuals.

Don't allow your bad emotions to ruin your connections. Through cognitive behavioral therapy (CBT), a learning-based treatment, a psychologist may assist you in becoming aware of your bad actions and how they influence others around you.

Sluggish Breathing

Shallow breathing is often seen as a telltale indicator of anger. Do breathing exercises if you start to feel short of breath. Your body's fight-or-flight mechanism, which is activated by anger, releases the hormone adrenaline. You may relax your body by practicing deep breathing.

Steps to get hold of anger

It's bad for your body and mind to be constantly troubled by your past and to lose control of your anger. Your mind may be requesting assistance via shallow breathing, violent outbursts, and feelings of malaise. You can control your rage. The first step to recovery is realizing that you have anger management problems and are ready to take the necessary action to address them.

Nobody enjoys dealing with someone who is challenging. If we could simply stay away from everyone we don't like, life would be so much simpler. Life, however, as they say, occurs. You may have to collaborate on a project with a bothersome coworker. Or your worst adversary continues attending business gatherings and social events. Worst of all, you could learn that your most obnoxious relatives are attending dinner.

1. Be thoughtful before you talk

It's simple to say something you'll later regret when you're under the influence of emotion. Before you speak, take a minute to gather your thoughts. Permit those who are engaged in the issue to do the same as well.

2. When you're at ease, voice your worries.

When you're able to speak clearly, be forceful yet non-aggressive when you vent your dissatisfaction. Clearly and simply express your demands and concerns without inflicting harm or attempting to exert control over others.

3. Take a workout.

Exercise may aid in reducing stress, which can make you furious. If you see that your wrath is growing, take a quick stroll or run. Or spend some time engaging in some other fun physical activity.

Not just timeouts for children. During difficult moments of the day, allow yourself brief pauses. You could feel more equipped to manage what is ahead without becoming upset or furious if you have a few quiet minutes to yourself.

Work on fixing the problem at hand rather than dwelling on the thing that enraged you. Are you angry about your child's filthy room? Knock on the door. Every night, does your spouse arrive late for dinner? Plan your meals for later in the day. Or decide to eat alone a couple of times each week. Additionally, be aware that certain circumstances are just beyond your control. Regarding what you can and cannot alter, try to be practical. Remind yourself that becoming angry won't help and can even make things worse.

Criticizing or blaming others could only make things tenser. Instead, characterize the issue using "I" sentences. Be considerate and specific. Instead of saying, "You never do any housekeeping," try saying, "I'm disappointed that you left the table without offering to assist with the dishes."
It is a strong instrument to forgive. You risk being overcome by your resentment or sense of unfairness if you let anger and other negative emotions overpower happy ones. If you forgive the person who offended you, your relationship may improve and you both may be able to benefit from the experience.
Laugh to relieve anxiety
Laughter may assist in reducing stress. Use humor to help you confront the things that are upsetting you and, maybe, any irrational expectations you may have about how things should turn out. Though it might hurt sentiments and worsen situations, avoid using sarcasm.
 Work on relaxing techniques

Use your relaxation techniques when your temper starts to flare. Try deep breathing exercises, visualize a soothing scene, or repeat a word or phrase that is calming, like "Take it easy." To promote relaxation, you might also do some yoga positions, write in a notebook, or listen to music.

Know when to ask for assistance

It might be difficult to learn how to manage your anger at times. If you have anger management problems, get treatment. If your anger seems out of control, makes you do things you later regret, or negatively affects those close to you.

Meditation is beneficial

It's been said that the power of your subconscious mind is thousands of times more than that of your conscious mind. Through meditation, you may access this powerful aspect of yourself. It is said that meditation treats the psychological, emotional, and physiological causes of rage. Here, we talk about a handful of them.

Meditation is the top method for propelling your brain into the future and evolution's undiscovered cheat code. one in which rage is unnecessary. "Meditation is the flowering of the prefrontal brain to transcend the momentum of nature," claims Amit Ray. In a ground-breaking 2005 research, Harvard neuroscientist Dr. Sara Lazar discovered that the prefrontal cortexes of meditators had a remarkable amount of "thickness," "folds," and total "surface area." You are aware of how pushups strengthen your shoulders, triceps, and chest? The same is true for the brain during meditation. Some individuals who struggle with anger are experts at being excessively theatrical, emphasizing the trivial, and stressing over minor things. Fortunately, meditation helps us see things from a far wider angle.

You Can Handle The Impossible With Meditation. First, meditation can help you become considerably more emotionally balanced so that you can appropriately cope with it if the answer is unclear or does not exist. You may act the helpless one. You are the victim after all! You could get cynical, resentful, and miserable in life. Certainly, people have given up for far less. You can lose control of your rage and become a shell of the person you. Alternatively, you may become more mindful. You might reset your irritation through meditation as opposed to letting it build up over time. You always have the option of turning back the clock on your worry, despair, and dissatisfaction.

You may transcend the event rather than continue to live your life in the mental abyss. You may utilize it as a launching pad to achieve more than you had ever imagined. Feelings of inadequacy, helplessness, and powerlessness, which are the origins of rage, are replaced with assurance, self-belief, and a constructive outlook.

The idea is that, even for those going through really terrible circumstances, meditation elevates your level of cognition above anger. There are many methods to overcome almost anything, and you could even inspire others in the process. This advanced mindset is unlocked through meditation. The best way to access that limitless well of inner wisdom is through meditation. Not only does anger obscure the mind, but it also escalates out of control, leaving you with a bitter, sad existence. A clear, disgruntled, and hot-headed mind simply cannot provide the types of beautiful, creative ideas that meditation's simmering of the inner mind can. Sometimes a little subconscious thought is required to come up with a suitable answer in circumstances that would otherwise have you tearing your hair out. What else do you need to know before you find a quiet place, close your eyes, and explore your innermost thoughts?

Let Emotional Intelligence come into Play

Many individuals are unaware of the fact that when one emotion, like rage, is so unstable, the rest of our emotional experiences as a whole are also unbalanced. Increasing emotional intelligence may help with this. Utilizing all of our naturally occurring emotions to practice anger control effectively requires emotional intelligence.

Being as open and honest as you can with trustworthy loved ones, particularly when you are unhappy, can help you avoid anger management. You must express your ideas and emotions in a manner that permits an understanding of your perceived vulnerability as well as your wrath, even when you are quite angry.

People eventually feel secure and come to routinely anticipate it when there is a mix of honesty, trust, and closeness. At the end of the day, this is all that "trust" actually means, and without it, not much else is possible. It is essential to emotional intelligence.

It is crucial to acknowledge the unpleasant situation in ALL of its discomfort while processing it with yourself or a loved one. Use empathy to regulate your rage and let your innate emotional intelligence take over. Frequently, when we believe we have found a solution, we are prone to acting immediately. Don't give in to this urge! That will happen, but only when your Loved One requests input. Your spouse will most likely sense criticism if you "jump the gun" with the advice and either defend themselves or stop talking.

People with anger management issues often find it difficult to maintain close friendships. The answer is intended to be offered via emotional intelligence abilities.

Expressing thanks for your loved one's willingness to invite you into these genuine and intrinsically vulnerable areas may help you manage your anger, whether or not you agree with what they have to say.

The easiest aspect of this emotional intelligence skill is also often the toughest since, more often than not, we don't concur with all of our partner's viewpoints. And what about that? You're not required to! You have a choice: you may concur or be in a relationship. When someone's emotional intelligence is so limited that it cannot sustain balanced emotional experiences, they require anger management skills. In these situations, the more we can promote emotional regulation - rather than conflict avoidance or "people pleasing" - the more we can have empathy or compassion with Self and Loved Ones through difficult emotional experience(s).

Have you ever heard of the idea of unwavering love or unwavering respect? A balanced emotional message and/or reaction will convey that. And are you aware of the actions we are predisposed to do after encountering this? If you can envision it, then it is not to erupt in rage.

General Advice on how to Approach Situations and People

Don't try to completely disregard your feelings, even if you may be practicing showing the world your emotionless face. Even while maintaining emotional distance from someone entails keeping them at a distance, you must also be aware of your own emotions. If you are unaware of when someone is hitting your buttons, you cannot stop them. So pay attention to the emotional rollercoaster inside of you. What is this individual doing or saying that irritates you? You may take action to stop them from doing it again by being aware of what is happening inside of you, such as knowing when to disconnect. Find a strategy to allow yourself time to reflect before continuing.

We often fear talking to someone we don't like so much that our anxiety levels start to rise before we even enter the room with them. It may be all too tempting to overreact and leap down someone's neck or say something you might later regret when your nerves are on edge. It's difficult to rein in emotions after you've let them out of the bottle like a genie. Therefore, take a deep breath and tap into your inner Zen if you know you'll be interacting with someone who makes you anxious. Calm your thoughts. Take a "let it go" mentality. If you see your temper starting to flare up, concentrate on speaking less and listening more. Never forget that you don't have to swallow words you never speak.

An essential leadership trait is being able to see things from others' viewpoints. After all, managers and leaders are expected to supervise individuals with various backgrounds. It doesn't matter whether you like your workers or not from the perspective of getting the greatest performance out of them, and it doesn't matter if they like you either. Seeking out the opinions of others with radically different viewpoints may be beneficial. They could have unique perspectives that push boundaries and encourage fresh ideas.

No matter who you are working with, a decent rule of thumb is to provide common courtesy to everyone. Even when you disagree, being kind and respectful to everyone will provide a foundation for civility. That entails treating others as you would want to be treated. Small acts of kindness may go a long way toward reducing tensions and building trust.

Put on your finest demeanor and concentrate on responding to circumstances with elegance and composure. People will respect you and see you as having integrity if you do this. You'll have the upper hand when interacting with individuals who seek to bring you down if you stay away from personal assaults and continuously behave with decorum. In actuality, navigating a minefield while dealing with a tough individual may be quite similar. For instance, you could be aware of a person's sensitivity to a certain subject. If so, it may be advisable to avoid having particular talks. Yes, you should be allowed to express your concerns, and choosing your fights does not include completely avoiding conflict. However, you should be selective about what you choose to work on and when, since many of our issues are temporary and may go away over time. Think about the topics that are important to you and the ones that you are emotionally capable of handling. If someone brings up a topic that you know will make them or you angry, politely decline their request to continue the conversation for the time being. It's not always simple to maintain your composure, particularly when interacting with someone who makes you angry. It could be time to bluff your way out rather than attempt to outwit them.

Consider this a chance to hone your best poker face. You would take every precaution to hide your hand if this were a high-stakes poker game. You would be expressionless, displaying just what you wanted to. This is essentially how you emotionally remove yourself from someone, and it's a terrific technique to give yourself emotional room when things become tough. If you often interact with someone you don't like, it could be beneficial to attempt to change your perspective on them or at the very least, make less unfavorable assumptions about them.

So try to see it from a more neutral perspective when you notice someone displaying a certain body movement you would ordinarily think was directed at you. Because you no longer have the pessimistic outlook, you chose to read meaning differently. You could say, perhaps she's just considering something else, like how much work she needs to do. This new perspective can help you let go of little things and feel less irritated. Avoid trying to handle things on your own since it will simply make you feel alone and angry. Consider using a network of allies. You'll be able to express your frustrations and feel heard when you turn to a close group of pals you can trust.

A trustworthy coworker or mentor may be able to guide how to handle a particularly delicate circumstance at work. Even just knowing that someone empathizes with your situation might be comforting. Additionally, your friends may be able to help you see a difficult individual from a different angle. You may want to consider trying to spend a bit more time with someone who irritates you rather than ignoring them. If the person is on your list of the Top Most Annoying People, this probably goes against every fiber of your being. But if you spend a little more time getting to know them—perhaps by collaborating with them on a project—you'll better comprehend who they are.

You may view things from someone else's perspective by putting yourself in their shoes for a while, as the saying goes. You may develop more empathy and compassion for someone you don't like by taking the time to understand them. You could realize there are causes for why things are the way they are. Your ability to establish a connection with them will enable you to overcome those annoying communication barriers. You could even discover that you share more things than you first thought.

You may want to take a closer look at yourself if you're experiencing persistent problems with someone and are finding it difficult to comprehend why. Consider what it is about this individual that irritates you. Are you exaggerating a situation because of your sensitivity? We sometimes let jealousy get in the way. Could your behavior toward this individual be affected by resentment? It may also be simple to misjudge someone's behavior or infer hidden motivations from it. Are there any aspects of your own experiences that could be unjustly affecting how you see someone? It's important to be conscious of your prejudices and preconceptions. The first step toward solving an issue can be admitting that you're somewhat at fault.

It's important to figure out a means to quietly but assertively convey your feelings if you're dealing with someone who consistently makes you break out in hives. The majority of issues are caused by the way we interact with one another. Try expressing how you feel in a non-confrontational tone rather than responding, which often results in overreacting. After that, listen to the other person's response. Be precise about the actions that irritate you and what you want them to do to resolve the issue. After you've stated your case, pay attention to what they have to say.

The fact is that you are solely in charge of yourself and your behavior. Focus on your approach to dealing with them rather than how much you detest someone or how furious they make you feel. Consider your options for preventing them from gaining your ire. Don't let yourself be a victim of someone who makes you uncomfortable. They are not worth the cost. Keep in mind that until you allow them, no one can bring you down or take your pleasure.

Chapter 3: Caging Hate

Hate is an extreme emotion of antagonism and aversion that often results from fear, rage, or an experience of damage. It is a strong aversion or revulsion. Everyone has felt and experienced hatred at some time, particularly after being deceived or having one's bodily or emotional needs violated. It's natural to sometimes feel hateful. Blame is at the core of all hate, and this is especially true of hatred that is directed outside of oneself. When one believes they have been severely mistreated or harmed by someone, their displeasure and indignation may contain the germ of hate.

Extreme hatred may incite violence, and harboring hatred for a long period can be harmful to one's mind and body.

The neurological, immunological, and endocrine systems are all adversely affected by hatred. Hatred may produce additional hate-related feelings. Both interpersonal and professional connections may be impacted. The chemistry of the brain is altered by hatred. Hatred also causes the mind to start speculating about potential defensive actions that the person being disliked could do. This worsens already present anxiety, agitation, obsession, and paranoia, all of which harm general mental health.

Stress hormones are released in the brain as a result of extreme emotions. These stress hormones gradually build inflammation throughout the body, which has negative effects on one's health.

Hatred has bred creatures out of men, women, and neuters. They began to enjoy hurting or causing suffering to their victims as a result.

Hatred is motivated by how we see the other, but it also has a close connection to who we are as individuals, with our past experiences and how they have affected our personalities, emotions, thoughts, and beliefs, particularly our sense of who we are. Hatred is fueled by two things: the ideology of the hater and the victim's devaluation.

These two elements both foster and spread hate. They lessen empathy because the target of the hate goes more and farther away from the hater. The hatred that grows against a particular person may ultimately be turned against the whole group to which that person belongs. Dehumanization of people or communities may result from this. Dehumanization is the practice of considering someone to be less than human, inferior, or cultured.

Dealing with Hate Emotion

Detachment of the mind and heart is the antithesis of hatred. Hatred produces a connection to the object or person it is directed towards. Hatred is a strong repulsive emotion. Hatred merely causes greater suffering since it erroneously boosts one's ego and causes one to feel very superior and righteous toward the object of their hatred.

People often disregard their hateful feelings or excuse them by blaming others. Negative emotions that go unresolved accumulate and worsen over time, having an impact on both the mind and body. The following advice may assist in overcoming hatred:

Recognize that you are feeling hateful. By accepting this, one may start to cope with this feeling and solve the issue.

Recognize the underlying causes of hatred. Fear, insecurity, or distrust are typical sources of hatred.

Never evaluate yourself against others. Instead, strive to be the finest possible version of yourself.

It is advisable to take a step back and refrain from responding quickly when you sense hatred. Making the proper choices is challenging when you are filled with hatred.

You could think about removing yourself from the scenario if you're experiencing hatred. The root of hatred is not a severe mental disorder. It may be brought on by past traumas and unsolved issues that individuals have harbored for a long time, but this is not depression.

Samir Shukla (2018) offers an intriguing viewpoint on how to end hatred: resist falling head over heels in love with anything and instead develop a logical defense for our decisions. In this approach, we may avoid being so devoted to one group that we start to disregard other groups. You can call it crazy, yet the writer's viewpoint makes some logic. Certain has said that whereas hatred is a complete catastrophe since it attacks both the guilty and the innocent, anger has some advantages.

Some Useful Advice

Always start by asking yourself why you believe an individual has harmed you. When evaluating why we should assess if the transgression was indeed severe enough to arouse strong hate for that individual. If not, this should be sufficient justification to ease the burden. Find the things that bring you joy and pursue them. Return to your yoga class and make lunch plans with your former coworker. Make the necessary efforts to regain your happiness so that you are not burdened by hatred.

Sometimes when we are angry, we see things through frosty lenses. Our attitude often changes when our whole perspective on a situation is altered. When your perspective on a circumstance changes, so does your heart's attitude. If you can achieve that, you will be more inclined to extend forgiveness and let go of the crushing weight of hatred. We are aware that losing a connection with someone you trusted might seem like losing a part of yourself, which makes it particularly difficult. But keep in mind that doing this also means you've cut someone out of your inner circle who likely didn't deserve it and didn't have your best interests at heart. You will have more time and space to genuinely live your best life now that this possibly poisonous individual is no longer a part of your life. Recover more powerfully than ever! You now have the room and time to repair the damage caused by that connection. Additionally, this implies that you have made room for someone deserving of your attention and affection.

The chemicals in your brain may alter if you pretend to be comfortable and happy for a long enough period. You'll eventually begin to feel what you're portraying on the outside and begin to genuinely believe it. When you see yourself focused on hatred or anger, stop right away and attempt to think of three things for which you are now thankful. You will have shifted your attention and let go of the hatred you were experiencing after your thankfulness list. You may now continue your day in tranquility since you have reclaimed control over it. You may repeat this as many as necessary throughout the day. The more thankfulness you cultivate, the less power hatred has over you.

Strong emotions are not often something that individuals want to keep to themselves. Write it down privately. Write your thoughts down privately before sharing them with your buddies for the umpteenth time. Write out your sentiments that you may not have been able to communicate to that individual directly in a letter addressed to them. It enables you to properly process your feelings in a secure setting while letting go of the burden of hatred.